PRIMARY COMPREHENSION
ART PROJECT BULLETIN BOARDS

Janet Dellosa

son

Table of Contents

The Purpose of this Book

This book is designed to help teach and reinforce the skill of following directions. Through the use of the comprehension art projects, the comprehension bulletin board border projects and the reproducible worksheets, students will find that reading to follow directions can be enjoyable!

What's Inside this Book

There are eight bulletin board sets in this book. Each set contains four features:

1. **A character that can be enlarged and displayed on the bulletin board**
   (See page 4 for specific directions.)

2. **A comprehension art project for the students to complete which reinforces the skill of following directions**
   Full-size patterns are included with complete student directions for coloring, cutting and pasting. (See page 4 for further explanation.)

3. **A comprehension bulletin board border project that provides further practice and reinforcement in the skill of following directions**
   There are patterns with student directions for coloring and cutting. The completed projects can be used to border the bulletin board. An answer key is provided on each bulletin board idea page to show the correct color coding.

4. **Three blank related reproducible worksheets that can be used for additional practice**
   The three types of worksheets are: color or fill-in, cut and paste and a decorated lined sheet. (See pages 5-6 for specific instructions for making and using the worksheets.) Completed worksheets can be used as part of the bulletin board display.

Example of a Bulletin Board Set:

1. Bulletin Board Character

3. Comprehension Bulletin Board Border Project

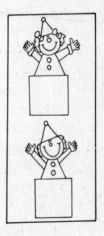

2. Comprehension Art Project

4. Related Reproducible Worksheets

How to Use the Bulletin Board Characters

A character has been provided for each bulletin board set in this book. Teachers can easily enlarge these characters to the size that will fit their bulletin boards by using an overhead projector. Using an overhead pen, trace the bulletin board character on a sheet of clear acetate. Tape a sheet of paper or tagboard to the wall. Place the acetate sheet on the overhead and project the character onto the paper or tagboard to the desired size. Trace around the projected image. Once the image has been traced, finish the sketch using the medium of your choice. Cut out the finished bulletin board character and attach it to the bulletin board.

How to Use the Comprehension Art Projects

A comprehension art project has been provided for each of the bulletin board sets in this book, with complete student directions for coloring, cutting, pasting and assembling.

The teacher may wish to make a comprehension art project with the entire class during the students' initial exposure to this type of following directions assignment. This initial introduction will provide the teacher with an opportunity to emphasize the following points:

1. Reading to follow directions can be fun when the assignment is to complete an art project.
2. Following directions is a sequential process. It is important to complete the steps in the proper order to assemble each art project correctly.
3. The skill of following directions is important because it is used daily. (This point may be emphasized by discussing why it is important to follow directions, i.e. following a recipe, putting a model together, learning the rules to a new game, etc.)

The projects may also be assigned on an individual basis or as a homework assignment for the entire class. The teacher can use the completed art projects for bulletin board displays.

Materials Needed:

1. scissors
2. ditto paper or white construction paper (If preferred, the art projects could be made from colored construction paper or from different colors and textures of wallpaper samples.)
3. crayons, water paints, poster paints, felt tip markers or chalk
4. paste, glue, glue stick or rubber cement

Answer Key

An answer key has been provided for each comprehension art project showing the formation and color coding of each project. The teacher should be aware that the art project may vary due to the angle at which the various patterns are pasted. The teacher may wish to explain this point to students during their initial exposure to the lesson.

How to Use the Reproducible Worksheets

A set of three reproducible worksheets has been provided for each of the eight bulletin board sets presented in this book. The skills have been omitted to provide the teacher flexibility in filling in the specific skills which the students need to practice.

Complete directions for making the worksheets using a thermofax machine are found on page 7.

Color Code or Fill-in Worksheets

Each of the bulletin board themes has one worksheet which can be used as a color code or fill-in worksheet. Following are some examples:

p. 20 fill-in
3rd grade
spelling: ee, ea

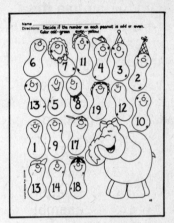

p. 48 color code
2nd grade
odd & even numbers

Cut and Paste Worksheets

A cut and paste worksheet has been provided for each of the bulletin board sets. Examples of completed worksheets:

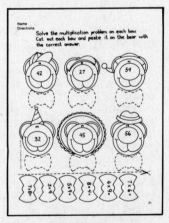

p. 21 cut & paste
3rd grade
multiplication

p. 42 cut & paste
2nd grade
rhyming words

Lined Worksheets with Decorative Borders

A decorated lined sheet has been provided for each of the bulletin board sets. These pages can be used in a variety of ways:

1. To write stories during creative writing lessons
2. To practice special handwriting activities
3. To take final spelling tests
4. To write letters for special occasions
5. To write thank you notes

Related word lists can be used in conjunction with these lined worksheets. The following are suggested ways to use the word lists:

1. Using the words in a story
2. Writing each word in a sentence
3. Writing the words in alphabetical order
4. Classifying the words into categories such as nouns, verbs, etc.
5. Using the words as a spelling list in addition to the regularly assigned words
6. Using the dictionary to find such information as phonetic spelling, syllabication or definitions

Word Lists

Ice Cream (pp. 9-15)	Bear (pp. 16-22)	Jack-in-the-Box (pp. 23-29)	Clock (pp. 30-36)
chocolate	fuzzy	toy	hands
vanilla	brown	music	face
strawberry	dancing	bounce	time
frosty	huge	surprise	hour
cone	grizzly	colors	minutes
scoop	growling	box	alarm
sundae	cub	handle	cuckoo
soda	paws	song	chimes
parlor	honey	melody	bells
cherry	claws	pop	winding
nuts	black	play	setting
frozen	woods	clown	watch
spoon	berries	buttons	watchband
dish	hibernate	nose	digital
whipped cream	parks	silly	grandfather
delicious	forest	funny	timepiece
sherbet	cave	enjoy	sundial
topping	polar	springing	pocket watch

Clown (pp. 37-43)	Elephant (pp. 44-50)	Television (pp. 51-57)	Sailor (pp. 58-64)
circus	peanuts	commercial	hat
bicycle	circus	set	boat
horse	gray	antenna	anchor
balloon	trunk	channel	ship
colors	tricks	program	uniform
funny	big	watch	bunk
stunts	jungle	comedies	ocean
dogs	African	mysteries	captain
laugh	zoo	adventures	shore
costume	cage	games	admiral
hat	heavy	news	seasick
nose	leathery	snack	deck
collar	tail	cable	fish
tumbling	mammal	schedule	navy
silly	snout	series	salute
dancing	tusks	cartoons	flag
jokes	parade	actors	mast
juggling	huge	actresses	sailing

How to Reuse Blank Reproducible Worksheets
Using Thermofax Machine or Photocopier

Materials needed: blank worksheet from this bulletin board set, sheet of lightweight paper, thermofax master, soft lead pencil, thermofax machine or photocopier.

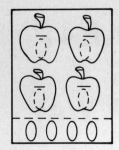 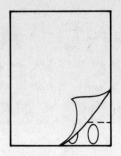 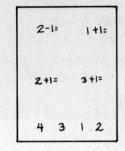

2. Using a soft lead pencil, fill in appropriate skills on lightweight paper.

1. Select a blank worksheet from this bulletin board set. Cover it with a piece of lightweight paper, matching edges precisely.

3. Remove lightweight paper. Using a thermofax master, run original worksheet through thermofax machine.

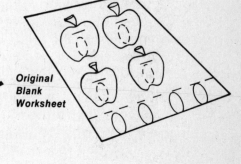

Thermofax Machine

Original Blank Worksheet

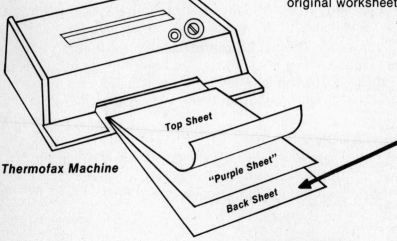

Lightweight Paper Completed in Step 2. (Skills filled in.)

4. Separate original worksheet from thermofax master.

5. Place lightweight paper completed in step 2 under the purple sheet in the thermofax master copy created in step 3. Match edges precisely.

6. Run copies in Step 5 through thermofax machine.

7. To make worksheets, use the newly-made thermofax master on a duplicating machine.

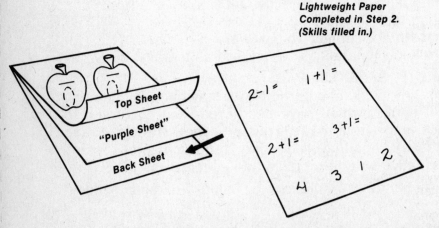

Reproducing Blank Worksheets Using a Photocopier

1. Make a copy of a blank worksheet on a photocopier.
2. Fill in duplicate copy with appropriate skills.
3. Make copies of completed duplicate copy using the photocopier.

"MAKE-IT AND TAKE-IT" WORKSHOPS
THE CARSON-DELLOSA WAY

Over 1,000 learning activity games available for teachers to copy

For a change-of-pace in-service session, try a "Make-It and Take-It" Workshop!
Call Carson-Dellosa Publishing Co. for information regarding several different types of "Make-It and Take-It" Workshops which are available.

Elementary teachers preschool - 6, special education teachers, reading and mathematics consultants, teachers of the gifted and talented, curriculum specialists, principals, student teachers, PTA volunteers and aides can benefit from the ideas and materials presented at the "Make-It and Take-It" Workshops.

THE WORKSHOP PRESENTATION
A comprehensive audio-visual presentation is given during the morning session illustrating these points:

- organizing, storing, coding and classifying games
- keeping records of student progress
- individualizing programs
- implementing learning activities in the daily classroom schedule
- tracing and laminating techniques
- adapting games for different subject and skill areas
- constructing bulletin board characters to be used as learning activities

THE "MAKE-IT AND TAKE-IT" SESSION
During the afternoon session, workshop participants may choose and copy from over **1,000** different games which have been organized according to specific skills. The games range from grade levels preschool through 6, and include the skill areas of reading (decoding and comprehension), mathematics, spelling, creative writing, English and economics.

Please write or call for more information on "Make-It and Take-It" Workshops:

Carson-Dellosa Publishing Co., Inc./P. O. Box 628/Akron, Ohio 44309
Call Toll-free 1-800-321-0943. In Ohio, call collect (216) 773-6885
Ask for the Workshop Coordinator

Super Duper Good Work!

Bulletin Board Border · p. 12 ► ►

The bulletin board border can be reproduced, completed by the students and displayed around the perimeter of the bulletin board.

Answer Key:
red - noses
yellow - top ice cream
brown - cones
orange - bottom ice cream

**Answer Key:
Comprehension Art
Project · pp. 10-11**
red - cherry
yellow - dish, base of dish
brown - top scoop of ice cream
orange - bottom scoop of ice cream

9

Comprehension Art Project
Ice Cream Sundae

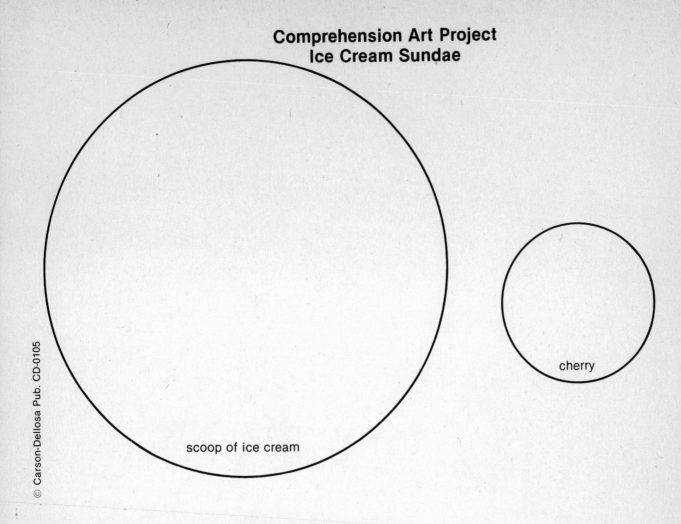

scoop of ice cream

cherry

Follow these directions to make the ice cream sundae:
1. Color one scoop of ice cream brown.
2. Color the other scoop of ice cream orange.
3. Color the dish yellow.
4. Color the base yellow.
5. Color the cherry red.
6. Cut out all of the pieces.
7. Glue the dotted side of the base to the dish by placing the base behind the dish. Make sure the dot does not show.
8. Glue the orange scoop of ice cream to the dish by placing the ice cream behind the dish. Make sure that only half of the ice cream shows.
9. Glue the brown scoop of ice cream to the orange scoop of ice cream by placing the brown scoop behind the orange scoop. Make sure that only half of the brown scoop of ice cream shows.
10. Glue the cherry to the brown scoop of ice cream by placing the cherry behind the brown scoop. Make sure that only half of the cherry shows.
11. Print the words **ice cream sundae** on the back of your sundae.
12. Print your first and last name on the back of your sundae.

Read over the directions.
Did you follow them just right?
Then go get some spoons,
And let's have a bite!

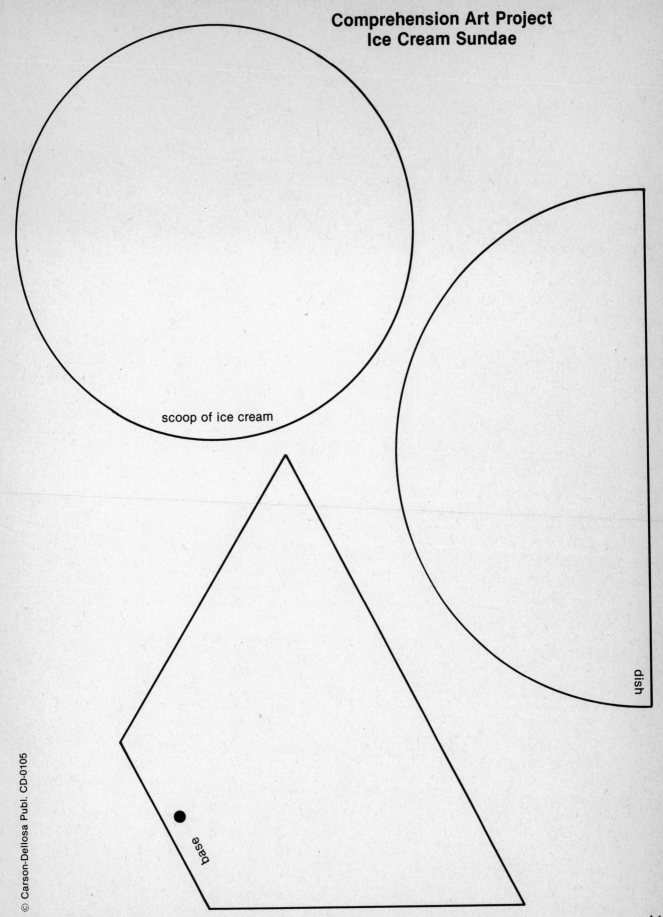

scoop of ice cream

dish

base

Comprehension Bulletin Board Border

Ice Cream Cones

Follow these directions to complete the top ice cream cone:
1. Color the nose red.
2. Color the ice cream yellow.
3. Color the cone brown.

Follow these directions to complete the bottom ice cream cone:
1. Color the nose red.
2. Color the ice cream orange.
3. Color the cone brown.
4. Start where you see the scissors and cut along all four sides on the solid lines.
5. Print your first and last name on the back of the completed sheet.

Name _____

Directions:

14

Name _____

Completed Bulletin Board Idea - Bear

"Bear"ers of Good Work!

Bulletin Board Border - p. 19 ▶ ▶

The bulletin board border can be reproduced, completed by the students and displayed around the perimeter of the bulletin board.

Answer Key:

Upper Paw:
yellow - claws
brown - bottom of paw

Lower Paw:
yellow - bottom of paw
brown - claws

Answer Key Comprehension Art Project - pp. 17-18

red - nose
yellow - inside of ears
green - bow
brown - face, body, tail, legs, outside of ears

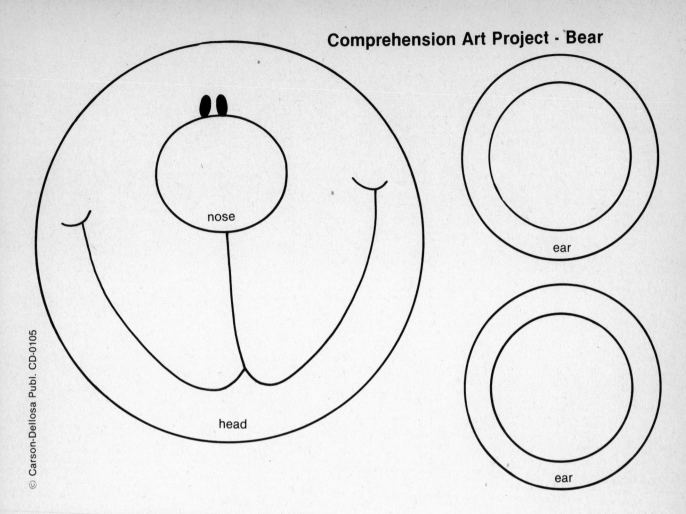

Follow these directions to make the bear:
1. Color the bear's nose red.
2. Color the head brown.
3. Color the body brown.
4. Color the tail brown.
5. Color the legs brown.
6. Color the inside circle on each ear yellow.
7. Color the rest of each ear brown.
8. Color the bow green.
9. Cut out all of the pieces.
10. Glue one ear to the upper right part of the head by placing the ear behind the head. Make sure only half of the ear shows.
11. Glue the other ear to the upper left part of the head by placing the ear behind the head. Make sure only half of the ear shows.
12. Glue the head to the H on the body. Make sure the H does not show.
13. Glue the tail to the T on the body. Make sure the T does not show.
14. Find the legs with the X's. Glue the legs to the bottom right part of the body by placing them behind the body. Make sure the X's do not show.
15. Find the legs with the dots. Glue the legs to the bottom left part of the body by placing them behind the body. Make sure the dots do not show.
16. Glue the bow tie to the body by placing the bow tie under the head.
17. Print the word **bear** on the back of your bear.
18. Print your first and last name on the back of your bear.

You did it, you read and you cut with great care.
Now see your reward is this very cute bear!

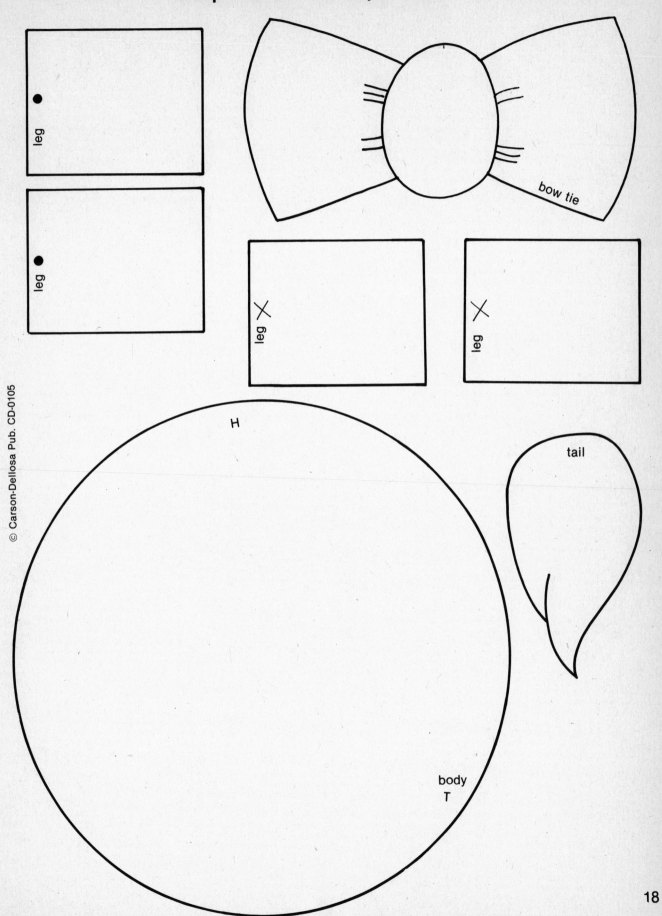

Comprehension Bulletin Board Border

Bear Paws

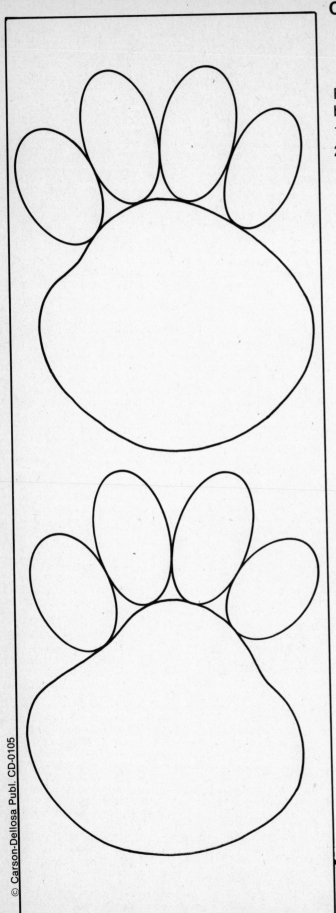

Follow these directions to complete the top bear paw:
1. Color the four claws yellow.
2. Color the rest of the paw brown.

Follow these directions to complete the bottom bear paw:
1. Color the four claws brown.
2. Color the rest of the paw yellow.
3. Start where you see the scissors and cut along all four sides on the solid lines.
4. Print your first and last name on the back of the completed sheet.

Name _____

Directions:

20

Name _____

Directions: _____

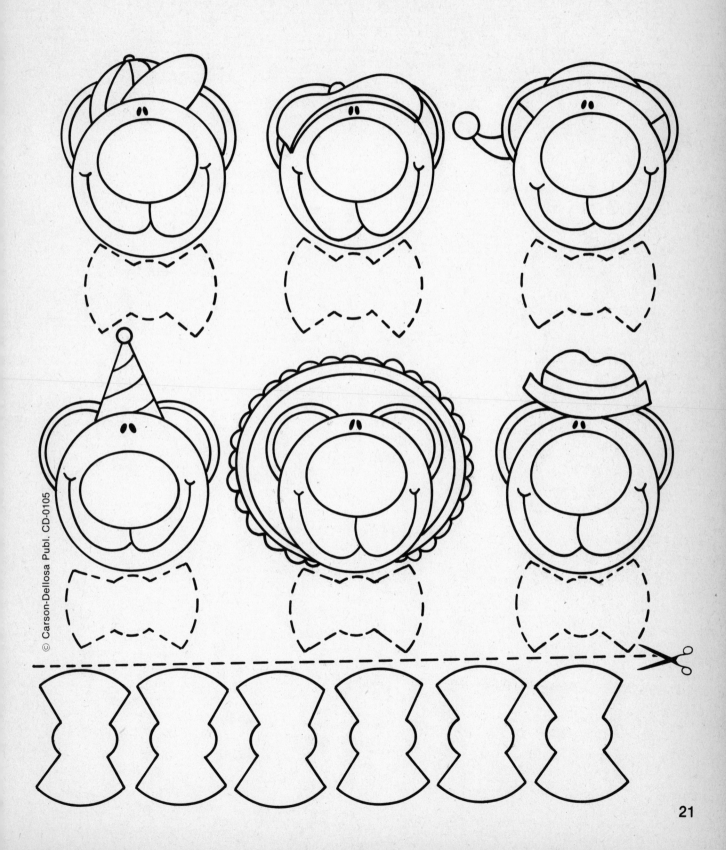

21

Name _____

22

"Popping Out" With Good Work!

Carson-Dellosa Pub. CD-8013

Bulletin Board Border · p. 26 ► ►

The bulletin board border can be reproduced, completed by the students and displayed around the perimeter of the bulletin board.

Answer Key:

Jackie-in-the-Box
red - box, nose
yellow - hat, buttons
green - hat top, hair bows, dress
brown - hair

Jack-in-the Box
red - hat top, shirt, nose
yellow - hair, buttons, box
green - hat

**Answer Key:
Comprehension Art
Project · pp. 24-25**
red - nose, hat, buttons
yellow - body, arms,
hat top
green - box

23

Comprehension Art Project · Jack-in-the-Box

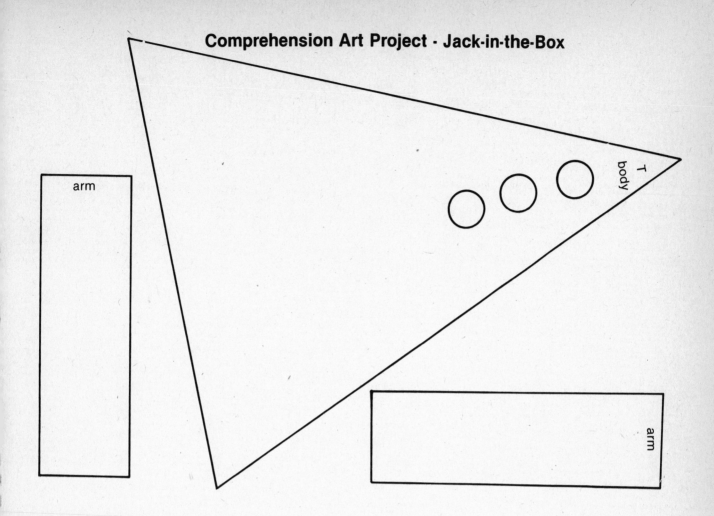

Follow these directions to make the Jack-in-the-Box:
1. Color the nose red.
2. Color the buttons on the body red.
3. Color the rest of the body yellow.
4. Color the hat top yellow.
5. Color the two arms yellow.
6. Color the hat red.
7. Color the box green.
8. Cut out all of the pieces.
9. Glue the hat top to the dot on the hat. Make sure the dot does not show.
10. Glue the hat to the top of the head.
11. Glue the head to the T on the body. Make sure the T does not show.
12. Glue one arm to the upper right side of the body by placing the arm behind the body.
13. Glue the other arm to the upper left side of the body by placing the arm behind the body.
14. Glue a hand to the end of each arm.
15. Glue the bottom of the body to the box by placing the body behind the box.
16. Print **Jack-in-the-Box** on the back of your Jack-in-the-Box.
17. Print your first and last name on the back of your Jack-in-the-Box.

Look what you have made all by yourself.
Isn't it fun to be able to read and follow directions?

© Carson-Dellosa Pub. CD-0105

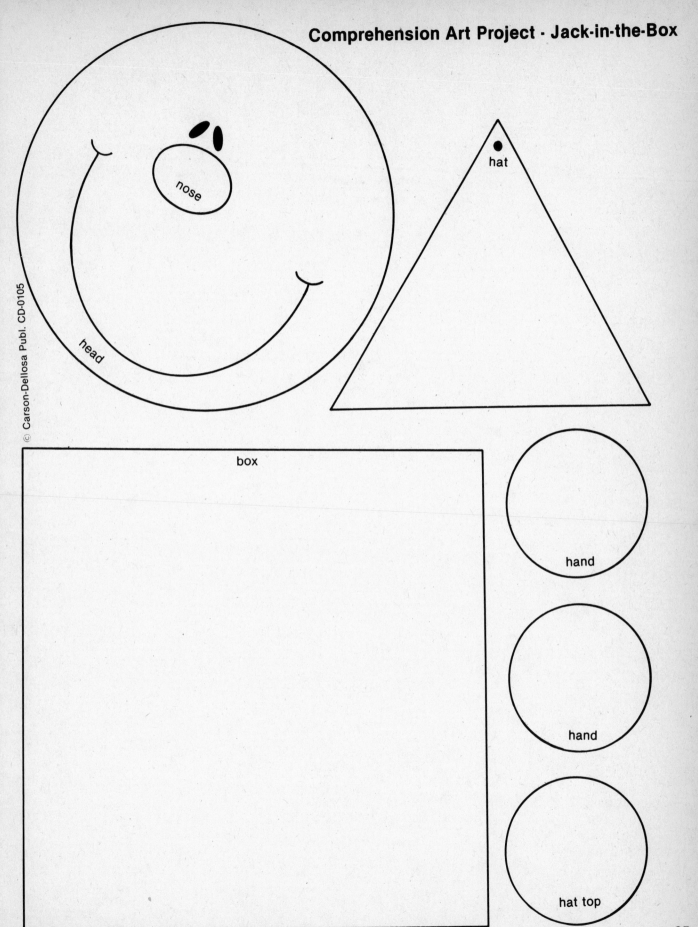

nose

head

hat

box

hand

hand

hat top

Comprehension Bulletin Board Border

Jack-in-the-Box & Jackie-in-the-Box

Follow these directions to complete Jackie:
1. Color the nose red.
2. Color the circle at the top of the hat green.
3. Color the hair bows green.
4. Color the box red.
5. Color the buttons yellow.
6. Color the dress and cuffs green.
7. Color the hair brown.
8. Color the hat yellow.

Follow these directions to complete Jack:
1. Color the nose red.
2. Color the circle at the top of the hat red.
3. Color the hat green.
4. Color the box yellow.
5. Color the buttons yellow.
6. Color the shirt red.
7. Color the hair yellow.
8. Start where you see the scissors and cut along all four sides on the solid lines.
9. Print your first and last name on the back of the completed sheet.

26

Directions:

28

Name _____

29

Tick Tock   Workers!

Bulletin Board Border - p. 33 ▶ ▶

The bulletin board border can be reproduced, completed by the students and displayed around the perimeter of the bulletin board.

Answer Key:

Bird:

red - bow
yellow - bird
orange - beak, feet

Clock:

green - clock rim, clock legs
black - clock hands

**Answer Key:
Comprehension Art
Project - pp. 31-32**

red - clock rim, clock legs

yellow - clock hands, top piece

black - small circle

(Times on clocks will vary.)

30

Comprehension Art Project - Clock

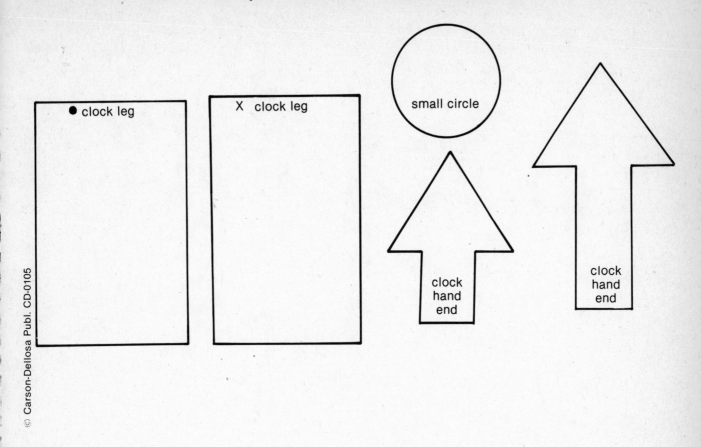

Follow these directions to make the clock:
1. Color the clock rim red.
2. Color the clock legs red.
3. Color the clock hands yellow.
4. Color the small circle black.
5. Color the top piece on the clock yellow.
6. Cut out all of the pieces.
7. Glue the dot that is on the clock leg to the clock rim by placing the dot behind the O on the clock face. Make sure the dot does not show.
8. Glue the X that is on the clock leg to the clock rim by placing the dot behind the P on the clock face. Make sure the X does not show.
9. Choose your favorite time. Glue the clock hands to the clock face to show your favorite time.
10. Glue the small circle over the ends of the clock hands in the center of the clock face.
11. Print the word **clock** on the back of your clock.
12. Print your first and last name on the back of your clock.

You should be very pleased with your clock
and pleased with your fine reading skills, too!

top piece

12
11 1
10 2
9 3
clock face
8 4
7 5
6

O P

clock rim

Comprehension Bulletin Board Border

Clock and Bird

Follow these directions to complete the bird:

1. Color the beak orange.
2. Color the bow red.
3. Color the feet orange.
4. Color the bird yellow.

Follow these directions to complete the clock:

1. Color the clock rim green.
2. Color the clock legs green.
3. Draw black clock hands on the face of the clock to show what time you like to get up in the morning.
4. Start where you see the scissors and cut along all four sides on the solid lines.
5. Print the time you like to go to bed on the back of this paper.
6. Print your first and last name on the back of the completed sheet.

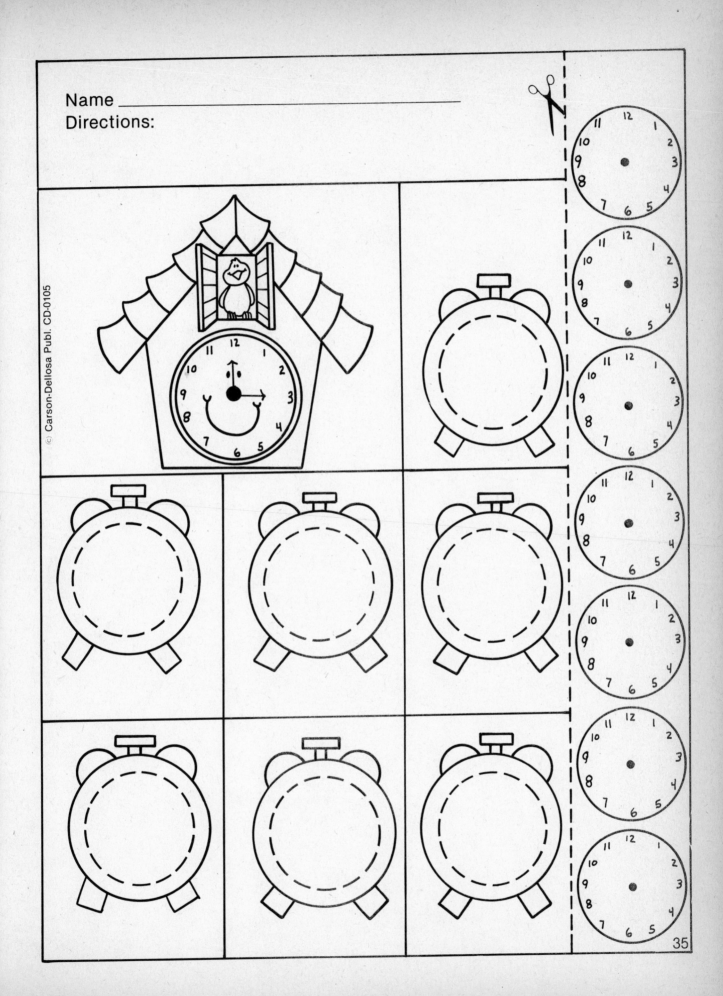

Name _____

Directions:

35

Name _____

_____

_____

_____

_____

_____

_____

_____

_____

_____

_____

Carson-Dellosa Pub. CD-0105

Good Work!

Bulletin Board Border · p. 40 ▶ ▶

The bulletin board border can be reproduced, completed by the students and displayed around the perimeter of the bulletin board.

Answer Key:
red - all noses
yellow - bear balloon
blue - bottom right balloon
green - bottom left balloon
orange - long balloon

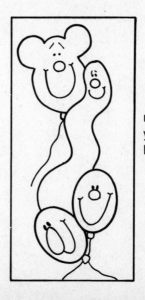

**Answer Key:
Comprehension Art
Project · pp. 38-39**
red - nose, hat top
yellow - hair, collar
blue - hat

Comprehension Art Project - Clown

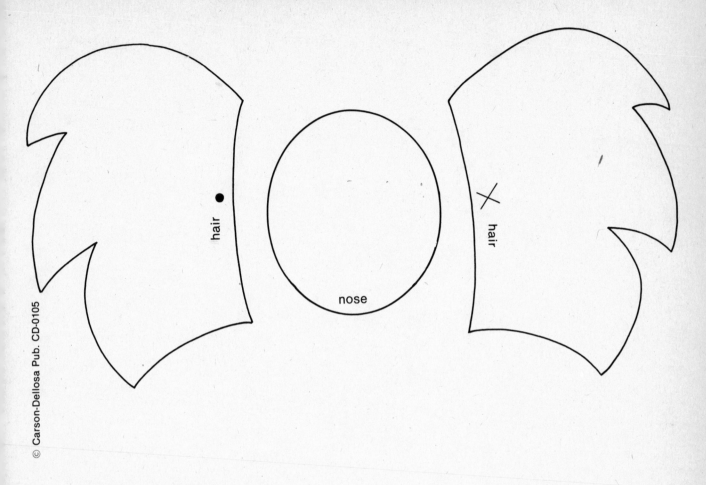

Follow these directions to make the clown:
1. Color the nose red.
2. Color both pieces of the hair yellow.
3. Color the hat top red.
4. Color the hat blue.
5. Color the collar yellow.
6. Cut out all of the pieces.
7. Glue the hat top to the dot on the hat. Make sure the dot does not show.
8. Glue the hat to the top of the head.
9. Find the hair with the dot. Glue the hair to the left side of the head by placing the hair behind the head. Make sure the dot does not show.
10. Find the hair with the X. Glue the hair to the right side of the head by placing the hair behind the head. Make sure the X does not show.
11. Glue the nose under the eyes.
12. Glue the straight side of the collar to the bottom of the head by placing the collar behind the head.
13. Print the word **clown** on the back of your clown.
14. Print your first and last name on the back of your clown.

Aren't you glad you can read? Look what you were able to make by following directions!

Comprehension Art Project - Clown

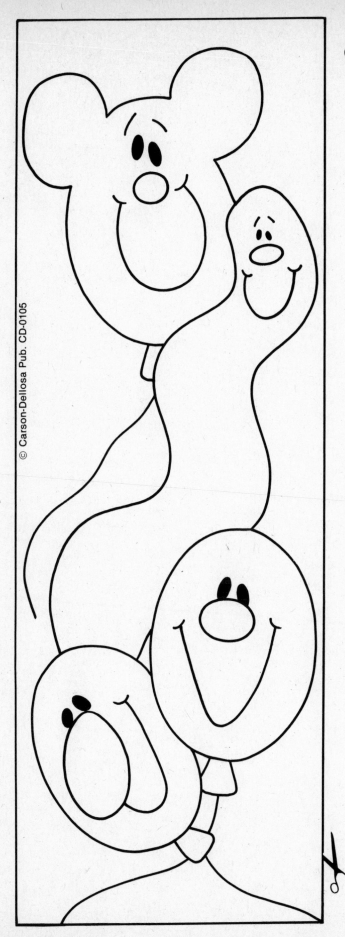

Comprehension Bulletin Board Border
Balloons

Follow these directions to complete the balloons:
1. Color the nose on the bear balloon red.
2. Color the rest of the bear balloon yellow.
3. Color the nose on the long balloon red.
4. Color the rest of the long balloon orange.
5. Color the nose on the balloon at the bottom right red.
6. Color the rest of the balloon at the bottom right blue.
7. Color the nose on the balloon at the bottom left red.
8. Color the rest of the balloon at the bottom left green.
9. Start where you see the scissors and cut along all four sides on the solid lines.
10. Print your first and last name on the back of the completed sheet.

Name _____

Directions:

41

Name _____
Directions:

42

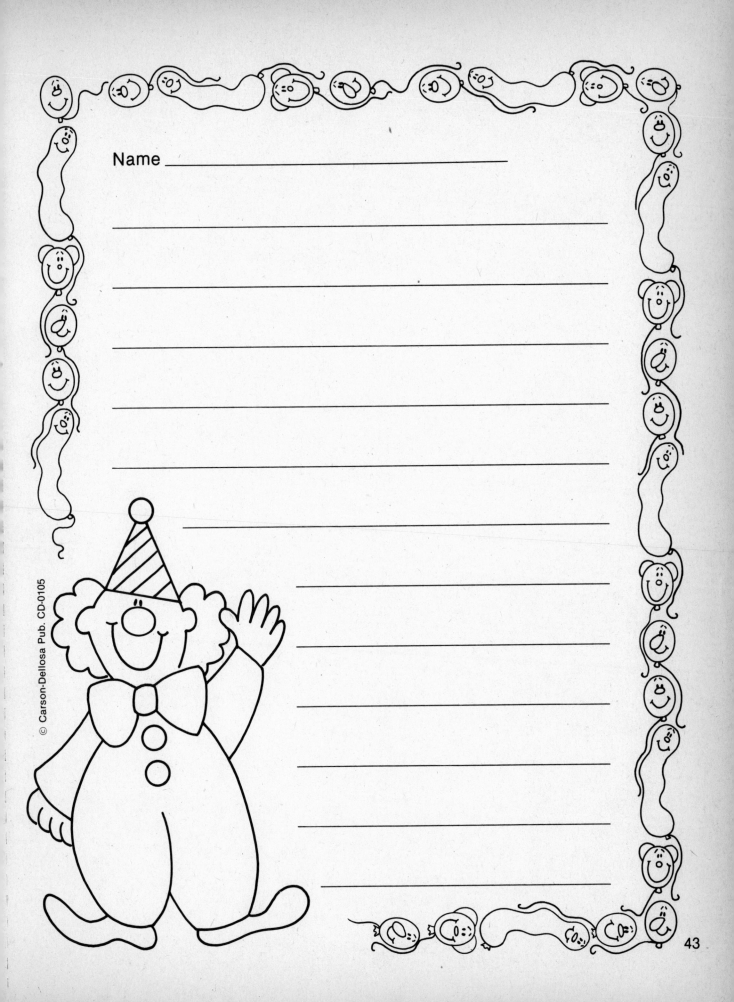

Name _____

43

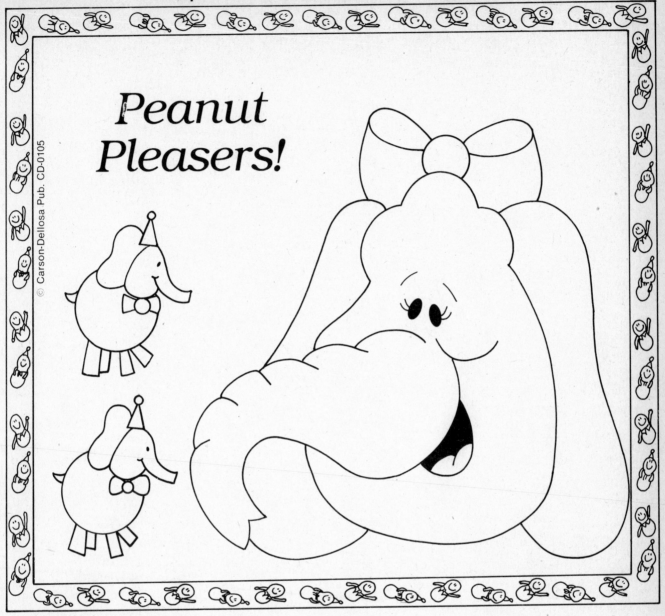

Peanut Pleasers!

Bulletin Board Border · p. 47

The bulletin board border can be reproduced, completed by the students and displayed around the perimeter of the bulletin board.

Answer Key:

Top Peanut:
red · collar
yellow · face, body, arms and hands
blue · bow tie
gray · peanuts in hands

Bottom Peanut:
red · hat
yellow · ribbon and bow, peanuts in hands
blue · hat ball
gray · face, body, arms and hands

**Answer Key
Comprehension Art
Project · pp. 45-46**
red · bow tie
yellow · ball on hat
blue · hat
gray · entire elephant

44

Comprehension Art Project - Elephant

Follow these directions to make the elephant:
1. Color the head gray.
2. Color the body and tail gray.
3. Color the ear gray.
4. Color the legs gray.
5. Color the ball on the top of the hat yellow.
6. Color the rest of the hat blue.
7. Color the bow tie red.
8. Cut out all of the pieces.
9. Glue the ear to the E on the head. Make sure the E does not show.
10. Glue the head to the R on the body. Make sure the R does not show.
11. Glue the two legs with the X's to the bottom right part of the body by placing them behind the body. Make sure the X's do not show.
12. Glue the two legs with the dots to the bottom left part of the body by placing them behind the body. Make sure the dots do not show.
13. Glue the hat to the top of the head.
14. Glue the bow tie to the body by placing the bow tie under the head.
15. Print the word **elephant** on the back of your elephant.
16. Print your first and last name on the back of your elephant.

Do you know why your elephant looks so nice? You read the directions and followed them carefully.

45

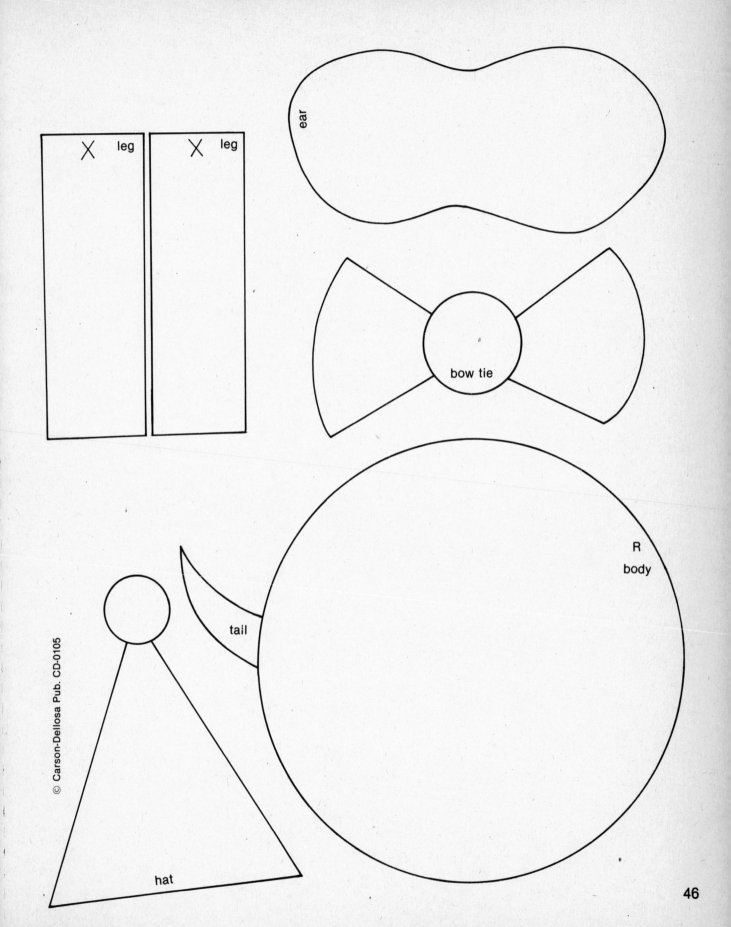

Comprehension Bulletin Board Border
Peanuts

Follow these directions to complete the top peanut:
1. Color the collar red.
2. Color the bow tie blue.
3. Color the face yellow.
4. Color the body yellow.
5. Color the peanut in each hand gray.
6. Color the arms and hands yellow.

Follow these directions to complete the bottom peanut:
1. Color the ribbon and bow yellow.
2. Color the ball on the top of the hat blue.
3. Color the hat red.
4. Color the face gray.
5. Color the body gray.
6. Color the peanut in each hand yellow.
7. Color the arms and hands gray.
8. Start where you see the scissors and cut along all four sides on the solid lines.
8. Print your first and last name on the back of the completed sheet.

Name ____________________________________

Directions:

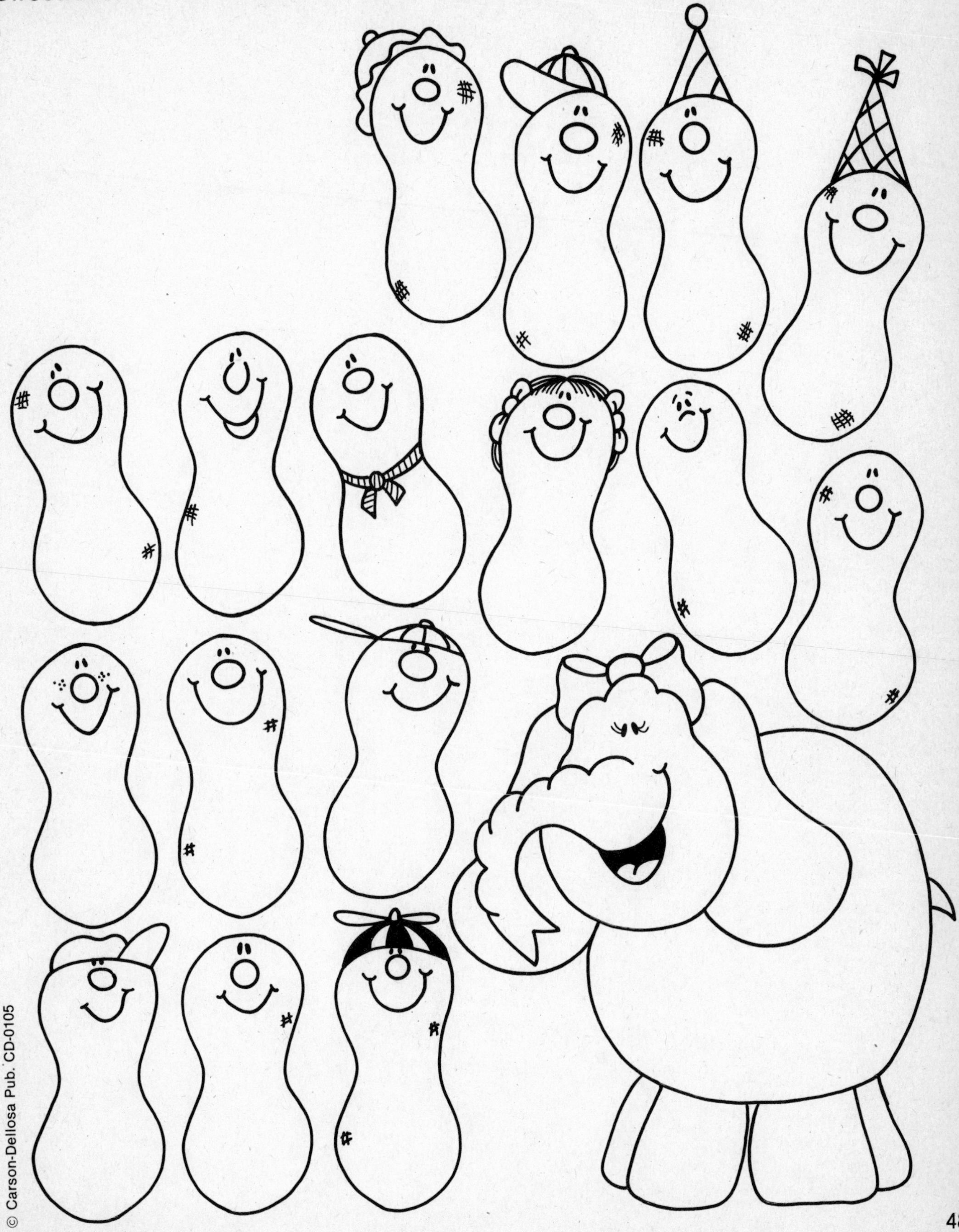

Name _____

Directions:

49

Name _____

_____

_____

_____

_____

_____

_____

_____

_____

_____

_____

Completed Bulletin Board Idea - Television

TV Stars!

Bulletin Board Border · p. 54 ▶ ▶

The bulletin board border can be reproduced, completed by the students and displayed around the perimeter of the bulletin board.

**Answer Key:
Top Television:**

yellow - antenna (except for circles), circles below screen

brown - antenna circles, television set and legs

Bottom Television:

orange - antenna (except for circles), circles below screen

brown - antenna circles, television set and legs

**Answer Key:
Comprehension Art Project · pp. 52-53**

yellow - antenna circles

orange - antenna, circles under screen

brown - television set and legs

(Pictures on the screens will vary)

51

Comprehension Art Project - Television Set

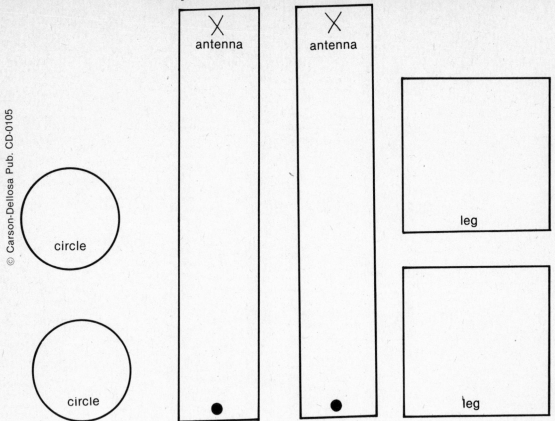

Follow these directions to make the television set:
1. Color two circles yellow.
2. Color four circles orange.
3. Color the antennas orange.
4. Color the legs brown.
5. Color the television set brown. Do not color the screen.
6. Cut out all of the pieces.
7. Glue a yellow circle to the X on each antenna. Make sure the X's do not show.
8. Glue the dots on the antennas to the top of the television set by placing them behind the television set. Make sure the antennas are in a V shape. The dots should not show.
9. Glue an orange circle to each X on the television set.
10. Glue one leg to the bottom right side of the television set by placing the leg behind the television set.
11. Glue the other leg to the bottom left side of the television set by placing the leg behind the television set.
12. Choose a character from one of your favorite television shows. Draw the character on the screen.
13. Color the picture on the screen.
14. Print the words **television set** on the back of your television set.
15. Print your first and last name on the back of your television set.

Turn on your set,
It's ready to go.
Isn't it time
For your favorite show?

Comprehension Art Project - Television Set

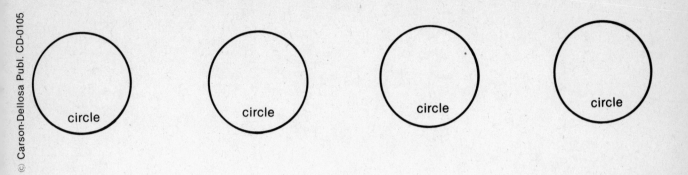

circle   circle   circle   circle

television set

top

screen

X   X   X   X

bottom

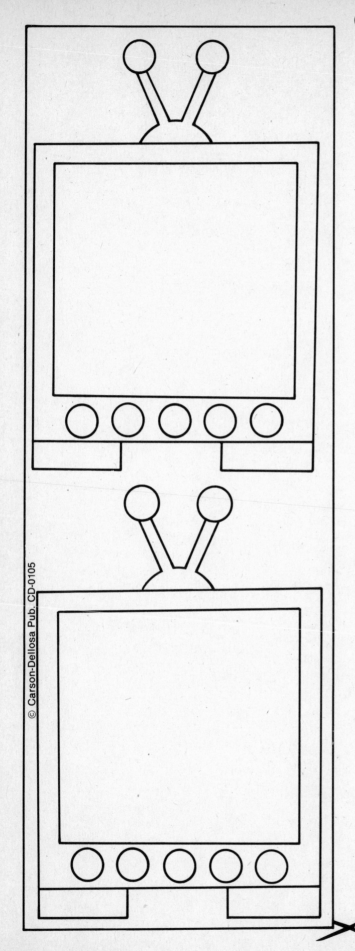

Comprehension Bulletin Board Border

Television Sets

Follow these directions to complete the top television set:

1. Color the circles on top of the antenna brown.
2. Color the rest of the antenna yellow.
3. Color the circles below the screen yellow.
4. Color the television set and legs brown. Do not color the screen.
5. Choose a character from one of your favorite television shows. Draw the character on the screen.
6. Color the picture on the screen.

Follow these directions to complete the bottom television set:

1. Color the circles on top of the antenna brown.
2. Color the rest of the antenna orange.
3. Color the circles below the screen orange.
4. Color the television set and legs brown. Do not color the screen.
5. Choose a character from another one of your favorite television shows. Draw the character on the screen.
6. Color the picture on the screen.
7. Start where you see the scissors and cut along all four sides on the solid lines.
8. Print your first and last name on the back of the completed sheet.

© Carson-Dellosa Pub. CD-0105

Name _____

Directions:

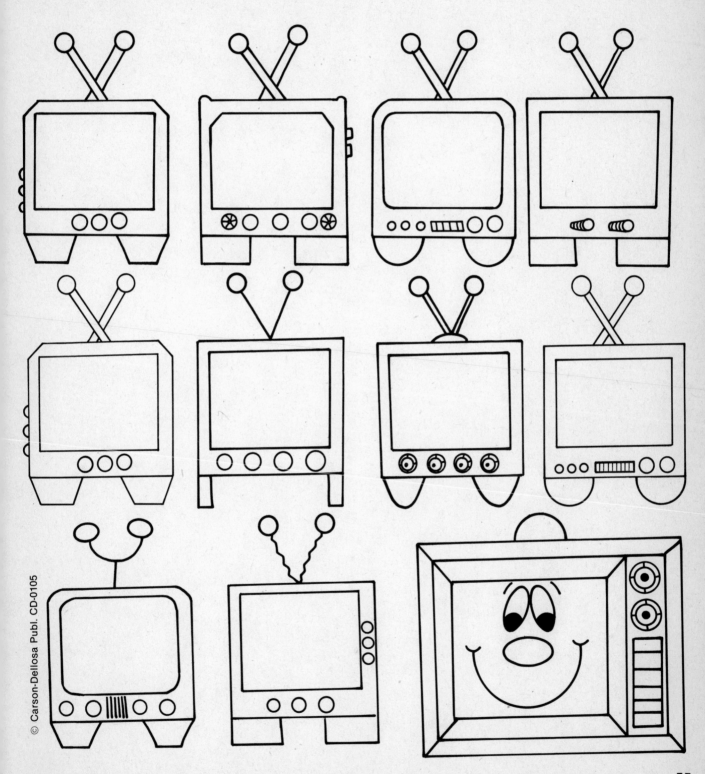

55

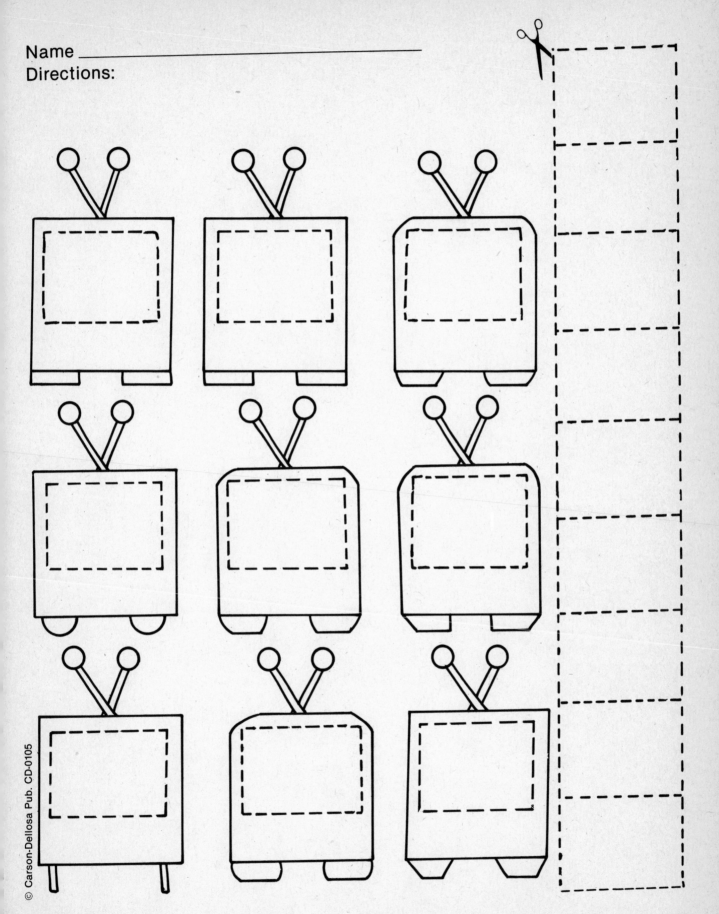

Name _____

Completed Bulletin Board Idea - Sailor

Ahoy!
"First Class"
Mates!

Bulletin Board Border - p.61 ►►

The bulletin board border can be reproduced, completed by the students and displayed around the perimeter of the bulletin board.

Answer Key:
Top Picture:
red - girl's shirt, flag, hair bows, boy's bow tie, boat
yellow - mast
blue - boy's suit
black - girl's hair, boy's hair

Bottom Picture:
red - toes on boy's shoes
yellow - anchor
blue - boy's suit

Answer Key:
Comprehension Art Project -
pp. 59-60

Students may paste the patterns at slightly different angles than those illustrated. This will cause slight varia- tions in the completed projects.

red - flag, nose
yellow - boat
blue - mast, arm

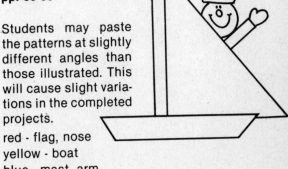

58

Comprehension Art Project - Sailboat and Sailor

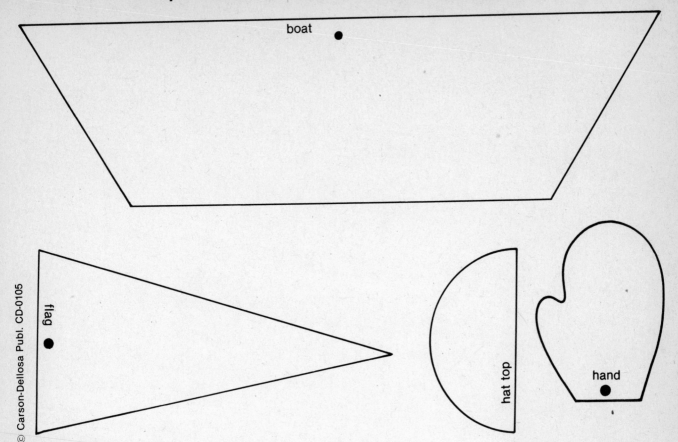

© Carson-Dellosa Publ. CD-0105

boat

flag

hat top

hand

Follow these directions to make the sailboat and sailor:

1. Color the flag red.
2. Color the mast blue.
3. Color the boat yellow.
4. Color the nose on the face red.
5. Color the arm blue.
6. Cut out all of the pieces.
7. Glue the mast to the boat by placing the X on the mast behind the dot on the boat. Make sure the mast is pointing straight upward. Make sure the X does not show.
8. Glue the hat brim to the top of the head.
9. Glue the hat top to the hat brim by placing the straight side of the hat top behind the hat brim.
10. Glue the head to the upper right side of the sail by placing the head behind the sail. Make sure most of the head shows.
11. Glue the arm to the sail by placing the arm behind the sail. Make sure the arm is below the head and pointing upward.
12. Glue the hand with the dot to the arm by placing the hand behind the arm. Make sure the dot does not show.
13. Glue the flag to the top left side of the mast by placing the dot on the flag behind the mast. Make sure the dot does not show.
14. Print the words **sailboat and sailor** on the back of your sailboat and sailor.
15. Print your first and last name on the back of your sailboat and sailor.

   Your new sailor friend says, "Thanks for the well-made boat."
   He hopes you'll join him for a sail.

59

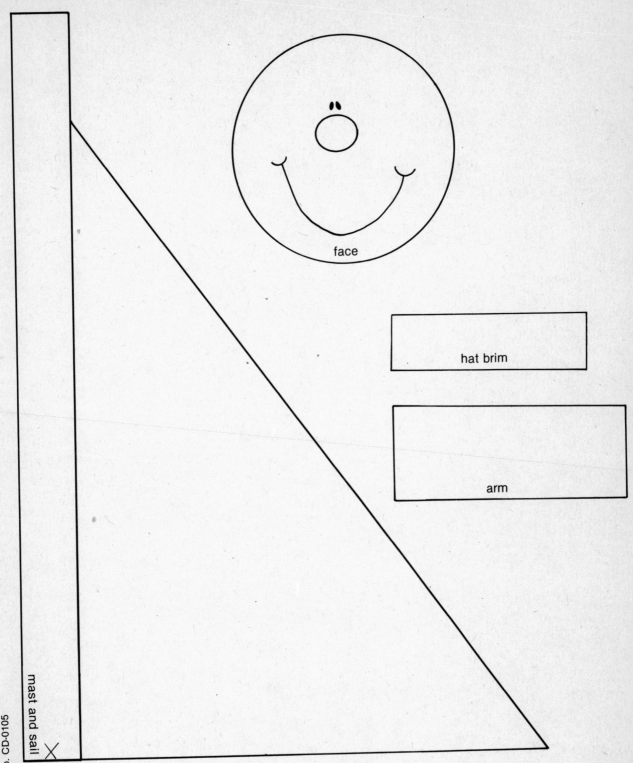

face

hat brim

arm

mast and sail

Comprehension Bulletin Board Border
Sailors

Follow these directions to complete the top picture:

1. Color the flag red.
2. Color the girl's shirt red.
3. Color the girl's hair bows red.
4. Color the boy's bow tie red.
5. Color the boy's suit blue.
6. Color the mast yellow.
7. Color the boat red.
8. Color the girl's hair black.
9. Color the boy's hair black.

Follow these directions to complete the bottom picture:

1. Color the anchor yellow.
2. Color the boy's suit blue.
3. Color the toes of the boy's shoes red.
4. Start where you see the scissors and cut along all four sides on the solid lines.
5. Print your first and last name on the back of the completed sheet.

Name _____

Directions:

Name _____
Directions:

Name _____